A Caldecott Celebration

Six Artists and Their Paths to the Caldecott Medal

LEONARD S. MARCUS

WALKER AND COMPANY

New York

For Amy and Jacob with love. —*L. S. M.*

First published in the United States of America in 1998 by Walker Publishing Company, Inc.
Published simultaneously in Canada by Thomas Allen & Son Canada, Limited, Markham, Ontario

Library of Congress Cataloging-in-Publication Data
Marcus, Leonard S., 1950–
A Caldecott celebration: six artists and their paths to the Caldecott Medal/Leonard S. Marcus.
p. cm.
Includes index.
Summary: Profiles six Caldecott award-winning books and their authors, including Robert McCloskey's *Make Way for Ducklings*, Marcia Brown's *Cinderella*, Maurice Sendak's *Where the Wild Things Are*, William Steig's *Sylvester and the Magic Pebble*, Chris Van Allsburg's *Jumanji*, and David Wiesner's *Tuesday*.
ISBN 0-8027-8656-1. —ISBN 0-8027-8658-8 (reinforced)
1. Illustration of books—Awards—United States—Juvenile literature. 2. Illustrated children's books—
United States—Juvenile literature. 3. Illustration of books—20th century—United States—Juvenile literature.
4. Illustrators—United States—Biography—Juvenile literature. 5. Caldecott Medal—Juvenile literature.
[1. Caldecott medal books. 2. Illustrators.] I. Title.
NC 975.M37 1998 98–6616
741.6'42'0973—dc21 CIP AC

Page 6: Jacket illustration from *Make Way for Ducklings* © 1941 by Robert McCloskey; renewed © 1969 by Robert McCloskey, used by permission of Viking Penguin, a division of Penguin Putnam, Inc. Pages 7-11: Drawings for *Make Way for Ducklings* © Robert McCloskey, used by permission of Viking Penguin and the May Massee Collection at the William Allen White Library, Emporia State University, Emporia, Kansas. Page 12: Photograph © Nancy Schön, used by permission. Page 13: Jacket illustration from *Cinderella; or, The Little Glass Slipper* © 1954 by Marcia Brown; renewed © 1982 by Marcia Brown, reprinted with the permission of Atheneum Books for Young Readers, an imprint of Simon & Schuster Publishing Division. Page 14: Photograph reprinted with the permission of the Archive of Charles Scribner's Sons, Manuscripts Division, Department of Rare Books and Special Collections, Princeton University Library. Pages 15-18: Illustrations from *Cinderella; or, The Little Glass Slipper* © Marcia Brown, reprinted with the permission of The Marcia J. Brown Papers, M. E. Grenander Department of Special Collections and Archives, University Libraries, University at Albany, State University of New York. Page 19: Jacket illustration from *Where the Wild Things Are* © 1963 by Maurice Sendak; renewed © 1991 by Maurice Sendak, used by permission of HarperCollins Publishers. Page 21: *Where the Wild Horses Are* dummy © 1955 by Maurice Sendak, courtesy of The Rosenbach Museum & Library. Page 22: *Where the Wild Things Are* dummy © 1963 by Maurice Sendak, courtesy of The Rosenbach Museum & Library. Page 23: Sketch for *Where the Wild Things Are* © 1963 by Maurice Sendak, courtesy of The Rosenbach Museum & Library. Page 24: Illustration from *Where the Wild Things Are* © 1963 by Maurice Sendak; renewed © 1991 by Maurice Sendak, used by permission of HarperCollins Publishers. Page 25: Mural © 1993 by Maurice Sendak. Photograph courtesy of Richland County Public Library, Columbia, South Carolina. Page 26: Jacket illustration from *Sylvester and the Magic Pebble* © 1969 by William Steig, reprinted with the permission of Simon & Schuster Books for Young Readers, an imprint of Simon & Schuster Children's Publishing Division. Page 28: Illustration from *Roland the Minstrel Pig* © 1968 by William Steig, reprinted by permission of HarperCollins Publishers. Letter © William Steig, reprinted courtesy of The Kerlan Collection, University of Minnesota. Page 29: Illustration from *Sylvester and the Magic Pebble* © 1969 by William Steig, reprinted with the permission of Simon & Schuster Books for Young Readers, an imprint of Simon & Schuster Children's Publishing Division. Page 30: Photograph © 1998 by Nancy Crampton, used by permission. Page 31: Jacket from *Jumanji* © 1981 by Chris Van Allsburg, reprinted by permission of Houghton Mifflin Co. All rights reserved. Page 32: Photograph reprinted courtesy of Chris Van Allsburg. Pages 33, 34, and 36-37: Sketches for *Jumanji* © Chris Van Allsburg, courtesy of The Kerlan Collection, University of Minnesota. Page 35: Illustration from *Jumanji* © 1981 by Chris Van Allsburg, reprinted by permission of Houghton Mifflin Co. All rights reserved. Page 38: Jacket from *Tuesday* © 1991 by David Wiesner, reprinted by permission of Houghton Mifflin Co./Clarion Books. All rights reserved. Pages 38, 41-44: Sketches and clay model for *Tuesday* © 1991 by David Wiesner, courtesy of David Wiesner. Photograph courtesy of David Wiesner. Page 40: Illustration reprinted with permission of *Cricket* magazine, March 1989, Vol. 16, No. 7. Page 45: Illustration from *Tuesday* © 1991 by David Wiesner, reprinted by permission of Houghton Mifflin Co./Clarion Books. All rights reserved.

I was very fortunate to be able to interview all six of the artists I have written about in *A Caldecott Celebration*, five
as part of my research for this book, and the sixth, Robert McCloskey, for an article published in the April 1992 issue
of *Parenting* magazine. I wish to express my thanks for their willingness to give their time and share their thoughts, and for the many kindnesses and
courtesies they graciously extended to me. In this connection,
I also wish to give my special thanks to Jeanne Steig.
My thanks to Susan Roman and the staff of the Association of Library Service to Children, American Library Association,
for their cooperation and help in making this book possible.
I would like to express my appreciation to the following individuals and institutions for information and insights shared and material made available for
use in this book: Mary Bogan, May Massee Collection, William Allen White Library, Emporia State University; Dorothy Christiansen, The M. E. Grenander
Department of Special Collections and Archives, University Libraries, University at Albany, SUNY; Nancy Crampton; Michael di Capua, HarperCollins
Publishers; Evelyn Diggs; Derick Dreher and the staff of
The Rosenbach Museum & Library; Andy Eskund, George Eastman House; Sheldon Fogelman; George Gilbert, American Photographic Historical Society;
Elizabeth M. Graves; Charles Greene, Rare Books and Special Collections, Princeton University Library,
Princeton University; Regina Hayes, Viking Children's Books; Karen Nelson Hoyle and the staff of the Kerlan Collection,
Walter Library, University of Minnesota; Holly McGhee, Pippin Properties; Municipal Art Society,
New York; Marjorie Naughton and Anne Deibel, Clarion Books; Doris Orgel; Jennifer Roberts, Houghton Mifflin Company; Morton Schindel and Cari
Best; Nancy Schön; Ginger Shuler, Judy McClendon and the staff of the Richland County Public Library, Columbia, South Carolina; Marc Simont;
Paula Singer; Lisa Van Allsburg; the Walker family.
I thank my editor, Emily Easton, for asking me to write this book, and for her wise counsel and attention to detail at every stage in its development.
I thank everyone at Walker and Company with whom I worked for their dedication, high standards, patience, and good cheer.

Book design by Claire Counihan
Printed in Hong Kong

2 4 6 8 10 9 7 5 3 1

Contents

★

★

Introduction

> It is deeply satisfying to win a prize in front of a lot of people.
> —E. B. White, *Charlotte's Web*

Artists, like everyone, enjoy being praised for a job well done. Since 1938, the Randolph Caldecott Medal has served as a public way of saying, "Excellent! Congratulations! You did it!" to some of the best artists creating illustrated children's books. Awarded annually by the American Library Association "to the artist of the most distinguished American picture book for children published in the United States during the preceding year," the Caldecott is a high honor for the winner. It is also a sign to readers everywhere that the book bearing the gold-foil Caldecott seal is special.

The Caldecott Medal was named for the nineteenth-century English illustrator Randolph Caldecott, whose wondrously lively picture books set a standard that artists ever since have hoped to match. A century ago, American children grew up with Caldecott's *Sing a Song for Sixpence*, *Hey Diddle Diddle*, and other illustrated books imported from Britain. To encourage American artists to make picture books that were just as good, it was decided from the start that the winner of the Caldecott Medal would always be a U.S. citizen or resident.

Winning the Caldecott ensures that a book will remain available at libraries and stores for years to come, and that it will be read by vast numbers of children. It increases the chances that a book will be published in other languages and adapted for video or even as a movie or for the stage. A winning artist's income is sure to rise, and as the chapters that follow show, his or her life may also change in other important ways.

Who decides who wins? A committee of fifteen women and men—a different group each year—meet to discuss eligible books and vote on the winner. Because the committee does its work in strict secrecy, little ever becomes publicly known about why the winning book received the medal (or why one or more additional books were selected for the runner-up award, called a Caldecott Honor Book). Lack of the inside story doesn't stop everyone else, of course, from having their own ideas about the medal—why the chosen book won, or whether another book should have won. Passions run high—and that is all to the good. One of the best by-products of an award such as the Caldecott (and its older companion prize for authors, the John Newbery Medal) is that it prompts librarians, teachers, parents, and children to talk about books—to choose their own personal favorites and to sort out the reasons for their choices.

The six Caldecott-winning books you will read about here span the six decades of the medal's history. I have chosen one book from each decade, so that viewed together, the six offer an informal cross section through time of the American picture book. All six have enjoyed a far-reaching popularity with children, and each is the work of an artist gifted not just with cleverness and skill but with what Maurice Sendak has called "a firm, clear vision."

Books bearing medals have the look of things that have been with us forever. But the truth, of course, is that someone, sometime, had to draw (and probably redraw) the pictures and write (and revise) the words. Certainly, none of the six Caldecott books described in the pages that follow just happened. None started out polished and complete. You are about to meet the people who made them. And you are about to see six works of art as ideas in the making: sketches and scribbles on the way to becoming books that readers prize.

A Note About Dates

The Caldecott Medal is always given to a book published in the year just past. For example, *Make Way for Ducklings* was published in 1941 and was the 1942 winner. The dates that appear at the beginning and end of each chapter and in the listing of medals and honors at the end of the book all reflect the year in which the award was given. The dates that appear in parentheses within the chapters are the dates of publication.

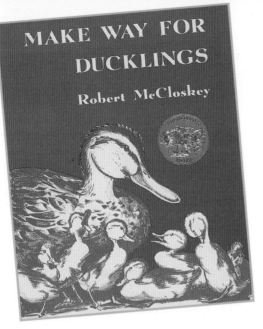

★ 1942 ★

Make Way for Ducklings

BY

Robert McCloskey

(born September 15, 1914, Hamilton, Ohio)

Publisher: Viking Press

Medium: lithographic crayon on zinc plates

> I spent the next weeks on my hands and knees, armed with a box of
> Kleenex and a sketch book, following the ducks around the studio and
> observing them in the bathtub.
>
> —Robert McCloskey, Caldecott acceptance speech
> for *Make Way for Ducklings*

Y ou have to rather think like a duck," Robert McCloskey once told a
friend, "when you put together a book like [*Make Way for Ducklings*]."

As a boy growing up in the midwestern manufacturing town of
Hamilton, Ohio, McCloskey played the harmonica, oboe, and drums and thought
about becoming a musician. Like his father, he also enjoyed tinkering with
machines; like his mother, he liked to paint. Happily for him, his parents encouraged all these interests.

McCloskey was a teenager when the Great Depression began—a time when money and jobs were scarce and when most people considered a college education to be a luxury. During his high school senior year, he won a scholarship to study art in Boston. But for that scholarship, McCloskey later said, he might never have left Ohio or become an artist.

During the depression, an artist had to be ready to do almost any kind of work. McCloskey tried his luck as an oil painter and watercolorist, as a muralist, and as a commercial artist. Remembering that a childhood friend had an aunt who published children's books in New York City, McCloskey went to meet the editor, May Massee of Viking Press. After looking at his portfolio, Massee urged the young man to keep drawing, hired him to illustrate a book jacket for Viking, and invited him out to dinner. That evening Robert McCloskey dined on duck.

May Massee was among the most gifted editors of her day. In that first meeting she had recognized the young visitor's talent and sent him away with good advice: to draw the things he knew firsthand instead of the stuffy mythological scenes that he thought a "serious" artist was supposed to draw. Three years later Massee published McCloskey's first picture book, *Lentil* (1940), with a story loosely based on the artist's own midwestern childhood.

As a student during the early 1930s, McCloskey enjoyed strolling in the Boston Public Garden, with its fanciful swan boats and resident families of ducks. By 1939 he had moved to New York. When a job brought him briefly back to Boston, it occurred to him that a story about the peaceful life of the garden might have promise as a picture book.

Dummy sketch for the scene in which Mrs. Mallard leads her children into the Boston Public Garden.

Without a definite story yet in mind, McCloskey spent hours in the garden, sketching and observing the daily goings-on. He had heard about a family of ducks that had stopped traffic as it made its way through the nearby streets of Beacon Hill. This incident, which had been reported in the local papers, was the story he needed! McCloskey wrote a picture book text based on the anecdote and sketched a dummy. Back

Two of the artist's many sketchbook studies of ducklings.

in New York, May Massee once again offered encouragement and agreed with the artist that he would need to learn a good deal more about ducks before he would be able to draw them well.

Over the next two years McCloskey studied mallard specimens at the American Museum of Natural History and discussed duck anatomy with an expert on birds. Still not satisfied, he bought some live ducks at the city market to serve as models. Sixteen ducks eventually came to live with him.

Also sharing McCloskey's Greenwich Village apartment at the time was fellow artist Marc Simont. Simont (who went on to win the 1957 Caldecott Medal for *A Tree Is Nice,* by Janice May Udry, Harper & Brothers) recalls, "[Ducks] wake up at the break of day and don't want you to sleep anymore either. They raised a terrible racket." The ducks ate a kind of feed called mash, which the artist brought home in big sacks. Because there would be duck droppings wherever the birds went, a good supply of tissues became another necessity. The ducks proved worth the trouble, however, as there was no better way for McCloskey to gain the thorough knowledge of his subjects that he needed.

The artist would want, for instance, to know what the underside of a duck's bill looked like when the duck was in flight. To find out, Simont recalls, McCloskey "wrapped one of the ducks in a towel and put it so that its head spilled over the couch. Then he lay down on the floor and looked up and sketched it." He made hundreds and hundreds of drawings.

Not all of the illustrations called for the same minute observation. McCloskey wanted the Boston Public Garden and surrounding streets to be immediately recognizable, but as the artist recalled years later, "It was never exact duplication but the *feel* of a place I was after." He did not try to draw the buildings of historic Beacon Hill brick by brick, but he did try to capture "the detail of the wrought-iron fence that a child would put his hand on or run a stick along as he walked by."

As he worked on the illustrations, he trimmed the text, letting the pictures tell more of the story. The story changed in other important ways, too. In the dummy version, Mr. and Mrs. Mallard live in Boston from the start and simply return home from their southward winter migration in time for the coming of spring. In the final version, the Mallards do not yet have a safe home in which to raise their family. Their search for such a home became the heart of the story—a story that everyone could understand.

Living with the birds prompted another change. In the dummy, McCloskey named the ducklings Mary, Martha, Phillys [McCloskey's spelling], Theodore, Beatrice, Alice, George, and John. In the final version, taking the real birds' squawking into account, he renamed the ducklings Jack, Kack, Lack, Mack, Nack, Ouack, Pack, and Quack.

McCloskey wanted to illustrate his story in watercolor, but May Massee would

Detailed drawing for the scene depicted on page 7.

Color study for the next-to-last illustration in Make Way for Ducklings.

not let him. The editor worried about the cost of printing a sixty-four-page book in color. (Color printing always costs more, and most picture books have half as many pages.) And she thought that as a young illustrator, McCloskey might do a better job without the added complication of color.

Spurred by his interest in machinery, McCloskey became involved in the mechanics of printing his book. After planning his illustrations on paper, he drew the final versions directly on sheets of zinc, a kind of metal used for printing. Drawing on zinc, which is a darker color than drawing paper, made it harder for the artist to see what he was doing. But working this way saved money and simplified the printing process. It also increased the chances that the printed illustrations would look just the way he wanted them to.

Make Way for Ducklings was published in the fall of 1941. Reviewers praised the book for its humor, warmth, and the sense of security offered to children by its story of a close-knit family. Weeks later the United States entered World War II, and in the months ahead the story's promise of security and a father's safe return came to mean a great deal to the children of a nation at war.

It was May Massee who telephoned McCloskey early in 1942 to say that *Make Way for Ducklings* had won the Caldecott Medal. The artist responded by asking her to tell him about the medal. Only four other illustrators had received the Caldecott. McCloskey had not yet heard of the award.

McCloskey entered the army the following year. After the war, his earnings as an author and illustrator made it possible for him, his wife, and their young daughter to move to an island off the Maine coast. Their life together there became the subject of later picture books, starting with *Blueberries for Sal* (1948).

Make Way for Ducklings went on to become one of the best loved of all American picture books, as well as one of the children's books most closely

Detailed drawing of the scene in which Mr. and Mrs. Mallard, in search of a new home, fly over the Massachusetts State House on Boston's Beacon Hill.

Make Way for Ducklings, *a bronze sculpture by Nancy Schön in the Boston Public Garden, has become one of the city's best-loved landmarks.*

identified with any American locale. In 1987, the year of the Boston Public Garden's 150th anniversary, a bronze sculpture of Mrs. Mallard and her children was placed in the garden in celebration of the gentle story that had become inseparably linked to the image and life of Boston. The sculpture was designed to encourage young children to climb on it. Four years later a duplicate was shipped to Moscow and installed in a public park as a gift "given in love and friendship to the children of the Soviet Union on behalf of the children of the United States."

Boston's ducklings sculpture was the idea of readers and fans. Although happy with the result, McCloskey himself has never been eager to see his story turned into anything other than the well-made book with which it began. He has refused several offers of a television series about the Mallard family. As the artist told a reporter in 1991, the year that *Make Way for Ducklings* turned fifty, "I think television has too much of its own way. . . . I tell them . . . it is better left as a book . . . and I'm pleased to see that the book remains."

1942 *Make Way for Ducklings* (Viking Press), Caldecott Medal

1949 *Blueberries for Sal* (Viking Press), Caldecott Honor Book

1953 *One Morning in Maine* (Viking Press), Caldecott Honor Book

1954 *Journey Cake, Ho!* written by Ruth Sawyer (Viking Press), Caldecott Honor Book

1958 *Time of Wonder* (Viking Press), Caldecott Medal

Atelier Von Behr/Courtesy of Simon and Schuster

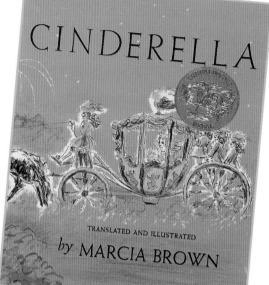

★ 1955 ★

Cinderella; or, The Little Glass Slipper

TRANSLATED AND ILLUSTRATED BY

Marcia Brown

(born July 13, 1918, Rochester, New York)
Publisher: Charles Scribner's Sons
Medium: gouache, crayon, watercolor, and ink

> When I was a child, thinking that I would like one day to illustrate books for children, I always thought of the fairy tales that I loved.
>
> —Marcia Brown, "Integrity and Intuition,"
> Caldecott acceptance speech for *Cinderella*

Growing up in a minister's family in upstate New York," Marcia Brown recalls, "we didn't have a lot of money. But we all loved books. Evenings and Sunday afternoons, my two older sisters, our Airedale, and I would all squeeze into our black leather Morris chair, and my sisters would read to me. We did it just for coziness, even after I knew how to read."

Brown loved to draw and to sing as a child, and she wanted to become either a book illustrator or an opera singer. Her parents, however, could not afford to pay for special training. When it came time for college, Brown was packed off to the tuition-free New York State College for Teachers in Albany to prepare for a "practical" future as a teacher of English and dramatics.

Brown could not, however, put one of her old dreams out of her mind. Three years out of college, she went to New York to become a children's book artist. She might as well have gone to a prince's ball. "When you're young and have come from a small town, as I had, New York looks like an amazing display of goodies—art, music, theater, dance—something wonderful to sample whichever way you turn."

By day she worked at the Central Children's Room of the New York Public Library. Free days and evenings, she explored the city, took art classes, and worked on her first picture book. *The Little Carousel* (1946) was inspired by a colorful street scene she had watched one day from her apartment window on Sullivan Street, in Greenwich Village.

When it came time to find a publisher, she decided to try her luck with what she thought was the best in the business. Viking Press—publisher of *Make Way for Ducklings* (1941) and James Daugherty's *Andy and the Lion* (1938)—topped her list. "But," Brown recalls, "New York just then was having an elevator strike, and Viking's offices were on the seventh floor. That was too many flights! Scribner's offices were on the fourth floor. So I climbed the four." Scribner's published *The Little Carousel* and went on to publish nearly all of Brown's more than two dozen children's books over the next fifty years.

Starting in 1946, Brown published a new picture book almost every year. And almost every year she finished as a runner-up for the Caldecott Medal—six times in all before finally winning the big prize

Bookshop and offices of Brown's publisher, Charles Scribner's Sons, New York. The ornamental cherubs seen on either side of the sign over the grand windowed arch inspired Brown's illustration of two similar cherubs (see page 17), one of whom tries to help Cinderella by turning back the clock.

for *Cinderella; or, The Little Glass Slipper*. In the late 1940s fairy-tale books were just coming back into fashion after years of neglect, and there were no good picture-book versions of many of the stories Brown had loved as a child. Having recently retold and illustrated *Puss in Boots* (1952) and *The Steadfast Tin Soldier* (1953), Brown next decided to try another childhood favorite, "Cinderella."

Brown now had to choose from the many versions of the famous old story—there are hundreds in all from around the world. The two best-known versions were those written by the Frenchman Charles Perrault and the German Brothers Grimm.

In the Grimms' bloodcurdling rendition, Cinderella's stepsisters chop off their

Page of research sketches depicting a royal guard standing at attention, a courtly couple dancing a minuet, and a high court official striking an important pose.

toes in a desperate attempt to make the glass slipper fit! Brown preferred the French version, with its loving fairy godmother, magical pumpkin-coach, and more forgiving view of human nature. "Perrault makes kindness the miracle. Those large, foolish ladies attempting to squeeze into a small shoe were drama enough, without cutting off toes. They were very human."

Brown revised her manuscript over and over until she had the strong, clear, fast-paced story she wanted.

Next came research. Perrault had lived 250 years earlier, during the last age of French kings. The ball where the young heroine meets the prince was a lot like the glittering parties the author himself attended at court. Perrault, in other words, had placed Cinderella at the center of his own fairy-tale world—and Brown wanted to show as much of that world as she could manage.

For three months the artist haunted museums and libraries, filling sketchbooks with drawings of hats, coats, hairstyles, fountains, chairs, beds, clocks, and slippers. She wanted to know how Cinderella and her fellow characters would have

dressed. She wanted to know how they would have *moved*. "People, you see, move differently in different periods. I was aware of this partly because I'm so crazy about ballet. The eighteenth-century flourish of a sword at the side and the skirts on the men's coats and the large dresses that the ladies wore all imposed a completely different physical look."

She knew she would not be able to put everything she learned into the book. But she also knew that "it would all be there in the background."

Then it was time to make the art.

"I start with very rough sketches," Brown says of the trial-and-error process out of which her illustrations have always grown. "As I continue to work, they get more and more refined. But then if they get too refined"—or begin to look too much like photographs—"that to me is death. There always has to be that little outlet for the imagination."

Compositional study, with characters cut out and pasted in place, for the scene in which Cinderella tries on the glass slipper.

She drew her characters on tissue paper, cut them out, and then rearranged them until they formed a pleasing composition. It was a little like playing with paper dolls.

She liked to work alone. Her editor, Alice Dalgliesh, was also a well-respected author. Dalgliesh helped Brown to get the text just right. Then, trusting in the artist's talent, she did her best to let Brown find her way without interference. "Knowing I had Alice's trust," Brown says, "was a wonderful kind of support in itself."

Looking at the stately Scribner Building gave the illustrator the idea for one of her drawings. An elegant, carved sign out front proudly trumpeted the old firm's name. Stone cherubs on each side looked as if they were getting ready to lift the fancy sign skyward. "In *Cinderella*," Brown recalls, "I wanted to have the cherubs holding back the clock, to give Cinderella as much time as possible!"

Cinderella was due to be published in the fall of 1954. That spring, Brown turned to the last important part of her job, readying her illustrations for the printer. This task was something like solving a giant puzzle.

Black ink and watercolor study for the illustration appearing opposite the dedication page.

Most people know that green is made by mixing yellow and blue, that purple is a mixture of blue and red, and so on. Change the shade of yellow or blue that you've started with, and a different shade of green results.

During the 1950s, as now, illustrated books were usually printed using no more than four standard colors of ink—yellow, blue, red, and black—no matter how many colors appeared in the art. Every color that the illustrator put into his or her pictures, therefore, had to come from some combination of the four. Printers had various methods, some involving the use of a special camera, for determining how the four standard inks should be mixed to achieve the best results. In the method used for *Cinderella*, Brown herself had to do the work of the camera, figuring out exactly what combinations and proportions of yellow, blue, red, and black to mix. It was a tricky, time-consuming job to "pre-separate" the colors—and Brown thoroughly enjoyed the challenge.

Once *Cinderella* was printed, there was nothing to do but wait, with fingers crossed, for the reviews. To Brown's relief, everyone seemed to love the new book.

Then, one evening in February 1955, Brown recalls, "I had been out for dinner, and when I got home there was a message to telephone Alice Dalgliesh in San Francisco right away." *Cinderella* had won the Caldecott Medal! Dalgliesh reminded Brown that she would have to keep secret her good news (as was still the Caldecott custom in the 1950s) for a whole month, until the official announcement of the award was made in March.

"People ask how it feels to win the Caldecott Medal. Well, how *would* it feel? It was *very, very* nice!" Brown went on to receive two more Caldecotts—for *Once a Mouse* (1961) and *Shadow* (1982)—more than any other artist.

Winning the award guaranteed strong sales for her book. "The first Caldecott

Souvenir folder designed and illustrated by Brown for the 1955 Newbery-Caldecott dinner, at which Brown received her first Caldecott Medal. The picture on the right (the front of the booklet when folded) is based on an illustration from Cinderella *depicting the prince's ball. The picture on the left honors the Newbery Medal-winner for 1955, Meindert DeJong's* The Wheel on the School *(Harper), illustrated by Maurice Sendak. Souvenir d'Amitié is French for "A Keepsake of Friendship."*

gave me enough financial freedom to go to Italy." She stayed for a year and a half, drawing, painting, visiting museums, and taking in her beautiful surroundings there and in France, Germany, Holland, and England.

"I've always believed that each story has needs that first have to be observed," Brown says. For this reason, she has mastered many different styles and methods of picture making—from the sparkling line drawings of *Cinderella,* to the strong, simple woodcuts of *Once a Mouse,* to the dramatic collages of *Shadow*—to suit the stories that have captured her imagination.

"It's been very, very lovely work," she says, "with a lot of freedom to do what I wanted. Very hard work, but that never bothered me. And I have done it with a lot of joy."

1948 *Stone Soup* (Charles Scribner's Sons), Caldecott Honor Book

1950 *Henry Fisherman* (Charles Scribner's Sons), Caldecott Honor Book

1951 *Dick Whittington and His Cat* (Charles Scribner's Sons), Caldecott Honor Book

1952 *Skipper John's Cook* (Charles Scribner's Sons), Caldecott Honor Book

1953 *Puss in Boots,* written by Charles Perrault (Charles Scribner's Sons), Caldecott Honor Book

1954 *The Steadfast Tin Soldier,* written by Hans Christian Andersen (Charles Scribner's Sons), Caldecott Honor Book

1955 *Cinderella; or, The Little Glass Slipper,* written by Charles Perrault (Charles Scribner's Sons), Caldecott Medal

1962 *Once a Mouse* (Charles Scribner's Sons), Caldecott Medal

1983 *Shadow,* written by Blaise Cendrars (Charles Scribner's Sons), Caldecott Medal

★ 1964 ★

Where the Wild Things Are

BY

Maurice Sendak

(born June 10, 1928, Brooklyn, New York)
Publisher: Harper & Row
Medium: india ink line over tempera

> *Where the Wild Things Are* was not meant to please everybody—only children.
>
> —Maurice Sendak, Caldecott acceptance speech for
> *Where the Wild Things Are*

The moment I heard the news I had won the Caldecott Medal, I rushed off to the florist, bought heaps of roses, and got into a cab. The roses were for my editor, Ursula Nordstrom. At my publisher's office, people were jumping up and down with excitement, and I can remember just hurling roses at Ursula. We were all so happy."

Maurice Sendak had first met Ursula Nordstrom thirteen years earlier. A shy but fiercely determined twenty-two-year-old when they met, he had grown up in

Brooklyn, New York, drawing pictures and making books and toys. As the youngest of three children, he was the baby of the family. He graduated from high school eager to make his mark in the world as an artist.

Sendak had a job decorating the display windows at F. A. O. Schwarz, the famous New York toy store, when Nordstrom saw his sketchbook drawings of city kids. The editor loved the drawings, and from that time onward she made sure that "Mr. Sendak" always had work as an illustrator. Nordstrom, who was old enough to be his mother, sometimes also made sure that on chilly days the young artist remembered to wear a sweater.

The editor chose many kinds of stories for him to illustrate: Ruth Krauss's playful *A Hole Is to Dig* (1952), the gentle stories of Else Holmelund Minarik's *Little Bear* (1957), and the classic fairy tales of Hans Christian Andersen, among others. She also encouraged him to write his own stories, starting with *Kenny's Window* (1956).

Sendak studied the children's books of the past. He hoped one day to create a book to equal the joyful picture books of the artist he admired most of all, England's Randolph Caldecott.

In Caldecott's books, words and pictures don't just tell a story. They have a lively presence of their own. Caldecott loved the sound and rhythm of words. For sheer drama, he sometimes put a single word of text on a page. A single word was often also enough to inspire an action-packed illustration. As Sendak once said, a Caldecott illustration "gallop[s] full-blast . . . at you."

In 1955 Sendak made a dummy for just such a picture book—then put it away to think more about later. He called his work in progress *Where the Wild Horses Are*.

Over seven years passed before Sendak returned to it. During that time he illustrated more than twenty books and wrote several books of his own, enjoying ever greater acclaim as an author-artist. He still had not created a Caldecott-style picture book, however. Then, in early 1963, he felt ready to try again. He began by writing a new version of his story every few days in a spiral notebook he carried around with him.

It was always going to be a fantasy, the story of a quest for something or someone faraway, mysterious, and wild. In one nightmarish version, a boy meets a stranger claiming to be his mother. When the boy refuses to believe her, the

woman turns into a fearsome wolf. The boy never finds the wild horses.

In another version, he comes to the right place, but he still can't see the horses—until he shuts his eyes! And in yet another version, the boy spends his whole life searching for the horses; when, as an old man, he finally gets within reach of them, he can no longer remember what it was he had hoped to find.

The story kept getting longer, slower paced. Sendak again put it away. "ABANDON!!!!" he wrote at the bottom of a page in his notebook, "dreadful story!!" But four days later he rewrote it once again. He showed his editor the manuscript "not frequently, but when I felt I was really going astray." Nordstrom sometimes knew how to solve a particular problem, and she always knew how to encourage the artist to keep trying.

On May 10, Sendak tried a new title—*Where the Wild Things Are*. While he continued to write, he also visualized the pictures he would later paint for his

1955 dummy titled Where the Wild Horses Are. *The pages of this handmade book measure three-quarters of an inch by seven inches.*

book. "I can compose and recompose in my head until an illustration becomes very clear, like a Polaroid," Sendak says. As the illustrations grew clearer in his mind, he realized big blocks of text were unnecessary—a description, for instance, of lush jungle foliage. What he could show with his illustrations did not also have to be said in words. After trying repeatedly to find the right words to describe the "rumpus" at the center of Max's adventure, Sendak realized that pictures alone could best tell that part of the story.

Sendak took his time before beginning to sketch and then paint the illustrations. "The minute I put down the first picture for a book as a sketch on paper, the sketch obliterates the image in my head," Sendak says. "So it is very important to start drawing at the right moment, with a firm, clear vision."

That moment came on May 25, when the artist made a second dummy, a miniature book measuring just two and one-half by three inches, with the text of *Where the Wild Things Are* in close to final form. By then Sendak had decided that the illustrations leading up to the rumpus would get larger and larger, as Max's emotions pushed out the words. Later in the book, as Max sailed home, the pictures would grow smaller and the words would take over again—as words do for us when we're feeling calm and well loved and able to think clearly.

Dummy of Where the Wild Things Are *dated May 25, 1963.*

Study in pencil for the scene in which Max begins making "mischief of one kind and another." Compare this drawing with the final art for this scene on page 24.

Sendak has compared making a book to making a soup with many ingredients that mix together in unpredictable ways. As the story changed, Wild Horses became Wild Animals, Wild Beasts, and finally Wild Things. Sendak had decided he did not draw horses very well; calling his characters "Things" also freed him to invent creatures from his own imagination.

The "boy" of the earliest versions became Kenny (the hero of Sendak's *Kenny's Window*), then Johnny (the hero of *One Was Johnny*), and finally Max. The "M" in Max linked the hero's name not only to "Maurice" but to that of Sendak's own childhood hero, Mickey Mouse!

A visit with friends whose son wore leopard pajamas to bed suggested Max's wolf suit. In early sketches, Max and the Wild Things look shy and underweight. In the finished illustrations, they have gained in both weight and confidence.

Like Sendak, Ursula Nordstrom was a perfectionist. They worried—and quarreled—about the text up until the time the book *had* to be printed, in early fall. The editor could be very persuasive. After absently calling the artist "Max Sendak," she began a note to him asking for a few small final changes by saying, "Maurice, or Max, or whoever you are—This is going to be a magnificent,

The stuffed toy animal on the left resembles Bucky, the teddy bear featured in an earlier book by the artist, Kenny's Window *(1956). Max has turned his back on the bear, suggesting a readiness for wilder companionship and adventures.*

permanent, perfect book. Bear with these last few questions, please!"

Where the Wild Things Are was published that October. Sendak wondered what people—especially adults—might think of his strange tale.

"There was no question," Sendak recalls, "that *Wild Things* was a book that was going to bump into trouble." He was right. Some reviewers feared that Sendak's toothy monsters, or his story about a mother who sends her child to bed without his supper, would scare children out of their wits. Some critics also feared that a book about a child getting angry at his mom might give other children ideas! Other reviewers, however, called the book a brave and daring work of art for children.

Winning the Caldecott Medal "meant everything" to the artist. Because the prize ensured that the book would sell very well, Sendak would no longer have to illustrate four or five books a year. "It made life easier, and it gave me the power to continue to do the kind of books I wanted to do." Like Max's story, Sendak's *In the Night Kitchen* (1970) and *Outside Over There* (1981) would describe the wild fantasies—and strong feelings—of ordinary brave kids.

Winning the medal also led outside the world of books. Composers came to

This forty-six-foot-long mural based on Where the Wild Things Are *serves as the dramatic focal point of the Children's Room, Richland County Public Library, Columbia, South Carolina. Installed in the room's garden atrium in 1993, the mural was painted by Michael Hagen, the scenic artist responsible for rendering Sendak's stage and set designs.*

Sendak, wanting to set *Where the Wild Things Are* to music. An opera based on the book followed, with a libretto written by Maurice Sendak, and then a ballet. A set of cloth dolls was made of Max and the Wild Things, and the characters reappeared in numerous posters and other images designed by the artist.

Not long after *Where the Wild Things Are* was published, Maurice Sendak received a letter from a feisty seven-year-old, who wrote, "How much does it cost to get to where the wild things are? If it is not expensive my sister and I want to spend the summer there. Please answer soon." Quoting from this letter in the speech he gave on receiving the Caldecott Medal, Sendak said, "I did not answer that question, for I have no doubt that sooner or later they will find their way, free of charge."

1954 *A Very Special House*, written by Ruth Krauss (Harper & Brothers),
      Caldecott Honor Book
1959 *What Do You Say, Dear?* written by Sesyle Joslin (Scott), Caldecott Honor Book
1960 *The Moon Jumpers*, written by Janice May Udry (Harper & Brothers),
      Caldecott Honor Book
1962 *Little Bear's Visit*, written by Else Holmelund Minarik (Harper & Brothers),
      Caldecott Honor Book
1963 *Mr. Rabbit and the Lovely Present*, written by Charlotte Zolotow (Harper & Row),
      Caldecott Honor Book
1964 *Where the Wild Things Are* (Harper & Row), Caldecott Medal
1971 *In the Night Kitchen* (Harper & Row), Caldecott Honor Book
1982 *Outside Over There* (Harper & Row), Caldecott Honor Book

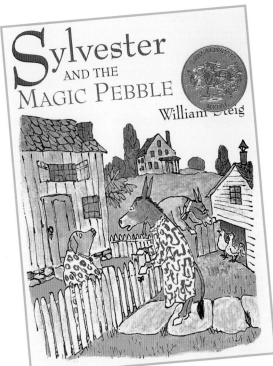

★ 1970 ★

Sylvester and the Magic Pebble

BY

William Steig

(born November 14, 1907, Brooklyn, New York)
Publisher: Windmill/Simon and Schuster
Medium: india ink and watercolor

[Art] . . . enhances the sense of wonder. And wonder is respect for life.
—William Steig, Caldecott acceptance speech for
Sylvester and the Magic Pebble

Why a donkey? You're going to ask me why?"

Ordinarily William Steig does not like to say too much about the books he has created for children since 1967, or about the countless drawings he has made, including many for the *New Yorker* magazine, since the 1930s. He thinks that a good story doesn't need to be explained. And he believes that artists don't always know why they do their art one way rather than another.

Even so, Steig has some idea why Sylvester Duncan, the hero of *Sylvester and the Magic Pebble*, his third children's book, *may* have turned out to be a four-legged fellow with fetlocks, long, pointy ears, and a tuft at the end of his tail.

"Donkeys," he says, "are my favorite animals. For some reason, every time I see a donkey I get pleasure from it. They're charming animals. They're like horses, but smaller. They're not overwhelming like horses. They seem lovable—though I never *had* a donkey. And they work hard. I like working people better than I like idlers, too."

Steig has worked hard for a very long time. "During the Great Depression, my father was broke, my older brothers had already married and left home, and my younger brother was just a kid. So it was up to me, at age twenty-three, to support my family. That's how I got into cartooning." He was soon selling cartoons regularly to the *New Yorker*, the magazine that every American cartoonist dreams of drawing for.

Born in Brooklyn, Steig grew up in the Bronx, the third of four sons. Both parents were amateur painters, and both were socialists. They taught their children to love beauty and to respect honest labor. Young Bill did cartoons for his high school paper, and when he decided a few years later to become an artist, his parents were pleased.

Ever since his childhood, Steig's favorite children's book has been *Pinocchio*, the story of a puppet that longs to become a living boy. At one low point of Pinocchio's fantastic adventures, he runs away from school. As punishment for his naughtiness, a pair of donkey ears magically sprout at the top of his head.

Steig wasn't much of a student, either. But as a gifted artist, he became famous for his cartoons, books of drawings for adults, and for the many advertisements for which he also drew pictures.

He never liked advertising. Ad work paid well, but using art to sell things did not feel right to him. Art, Steig thinks, should give enjoyment. It should be playful and mysterious. It should express true feelings and offer fresh ideas. When a publisher (and fellow cartoonist) named Robert Kraus asked whether he might like to do "a kid book," Steig replied, "Sure." At nearly sixty years old, he wanted very much to try something new and to escape from advertising.

Steig found he had a great many ideas for children's books. Kraus's Windmill Press published Steig's first picture book, *Roland the Minstrel Pig*, in 1968.

Illustration from Roland the Minstrel Pig.

"Drawing pigs is easy," Steig says, as if to explain how he chose his subject. That same year Windmill also published his *C D B!*—a sort of game book consisting of short sentences formed (as is the title) from letters that sound like words. For his next project, Steig wanted to tell another story.

The first thing Steig knew about *Sylvester* was that it was going to be the story of a donkey. He thought carefully about the story, and when he finally wrote it down, it hardly needed any work. But it needed a title. Steig made a list: *The Magic Pebble*; *The Pebble and the Rock*; *The Pebble, the Donkey, and the Rock*; and *The Donkey Who Became a Rock*.

He sketched a dummy and quickly made sample drawings to show his editor. (Unfortunately, neither Steig's dummy nor any of his early sketches for *Sylvester* have survived.) Drawing animals that behave like humans is always a bit tricky. How human should the animals be made to look? Steig was unsure at first whether Sylvester and his parents should stand upright or walk on all fours. He redrew Sylvester until the young donkey's expressions looked less like a grown-up donkey/person's and more like a child's.

Other details worried him. Steig wrote his editor, "I've been wondering how that rock should look. Sometimes I think it should resemble a donkey and sometimes I don't. One can't go wrong if it *doesn't* resemble a donkey, and one *might* go wrong if it does. On the other hand, it might add something if the kids can vaguely discern a donkey. It's a hard decision to make."

On October 6, 1967, Steig sent this note to his editor Robert Kraus along with a first draft of the manuscript for Sylvester. *The message reads:*
"Bob—A rough draft, written straight out & subject to correction & improvement, & my only typewritten copy (I have it also in illegible script). It looks good to me & I can imagine good pictures. I will learn to draw donkeys. Probably they should stand up like people.

All best   Bill   10/6/67"

Final art for the scene in which Sylvester realizes that the pebble he has found is not only beautiful but magical. "What a lucky day this is!" he tells himself—and then his troubles begin.

When he made his final illustrations, he first completed all the black-and-white drawings, then methodically painted in the colors one by one—all the reds, then all the blues, and so on. That way, he could be sure not to mix up the colors of his characters' outfits from picture to picture.

In *Sylvester and the Magic Pebble,* Steig told a story filled with strong feelings—feelings that in some ways may have mirrored his own at the time. The artist was divorced, and his young daughter Maggie had gone away to live with her mother. He missed Maggie, just as Sylvester's parents miss their young son when he's gone. Steig finished *Sylvester* in May 1968, just before Maggie was due to return home for a long visit.

Sylvester and the Magic Pebble was published in February 1969. Steig thought the printing had gone badly and was pleasantly surprised when friends liked the book anyway. Reviewers and fans of his work also delighted in *Sylvester.* And

Steig at his western Connecticut home, 1972. (Photograph by Nancy Crampton.)

when Steig heard the news that he had won the Caldecott Medal, he was overjoyed: Being chosen for the award encouraged him to feel that picture-book making—an art still quite new to him—had already become a good and worthwhile use of his talent.

"It's a good story," Steig says, browsing through a copy of *Sylvester* years later. "It seems to have some meaning. Don't ask me what it is!" But then Steig squarely faces the question, and gives his response: "The feelings are genuine."

1970 *Sylvester and the Magic Pebble* (Windmill/Simon and Schuster), Caldecott Medal
1977 *The Amazing Bone* (Farrar, Straus & Giroux), Caldecott Honor Book

Jan Bindas / Courtesy of Houghton Mifflin

★ 1982 ★

Jumanji

BY

Chris Van Allsburg

(born June 18, 1949, Grand Rapids, Michigan)
Publisher: Houghton Mifflin
Medium: Conté pencil with Conté dust

Dear Mr. Van Allsburg . . . I am so glad your books are so weird because I am very weird. I think you are weird but great.

—from a letter from a child, quoted by Chris Van Allsburg, Caldecott acceptance speech for *Jumanji*

A rhinoceros by itself isn't all that strange. And there's certainly nothing strange about a dining room. But a rhinoceros in a dining room is a very strange image."

For Chris Van Allsburg, a good part of the fun of being an artist lies in dreaming up such odd combinations in which ordinary things come together in surprising ways.

"Let's say I have some monkeys in the kitchen. How did they get there? 'They escaped from the zoo' isn't a very interesting answer. But as I poked around in my

Ball Coming to a Skidding Stop on a Checkered Carpet, *a sculpture in wood by Van Allsburg.*

imagination as I was beginning the book that became *Jumanji*, I finally thought: The monkeys sprang from a board game—a jungle game in which things come to life. Right away, that idea suggested all sorts of other possibilities for pictures."

As a boy growing up in the Midwest, Van Allsburg liked to draw, read *Mad* magazine, and play board games like Clue and Life. But his true love was model building. He spent many happy hours putting together model cars and planes, then imagining himself in the driver's seat or cockpit. His favorite childhood book was the story of another boy who liked to draw and daydream, Crockett Johnson's *Harold and the Purple Crayon* (Harper & Brothers, 1955).

In college Van Allsburg took art classes, at first just for fun, and found he had talent as a sculptor. "I liked making sculptures," he recalls, "that suggested there was a story to be told and that made people wonder, 'When was this made? Who could have made it? Why would anyone do such a thing?'" He went on to art school, and to a career as a sculptor.

Van Allsburg soon grew restless, however, and wanted to try new things as an artist. He began drawing again. He drew in black and white because he had not studied color in school. His wife, who was a schoolteacher, thought his clear, precise—and mysterious—drawings might appeal to children. So did their friend, author-illustrator David Macaulay, when he came by one day for a look. And so did Macaulay's editor at Houghton Mifflin, Walter Lorraine. After talking with Lorraine, Van Allsburg began work on his first picture book, *The Garden of Abdul*

Gasazi, which Houghton Mifflin published in 1979. That strange and fascinating book received a Caldecott Honor; many people felt that they'd never seen another children's book quite like it.

By the time Van Allsburg began writing his second picture book, he and Lorraine had worked out a routine. "I started by making an outline of my story," he recalls. "Then I made a list of the illustrations I thought would be needed." He and his editor discussed the story by phone. Lorraine would ask questions: "Can you tell that part more simply?" "Haven't you said that in another part of the story?" Van Allsburg needed an exotic-sounding name for the story's game, so he made one up: Jumanji.

With the writing done, Van Allsburg began to make "many, many, many, many sketches for each picture. Composition—the placement of the subject matter of a drawing within the rectangle of the picture—is the part of picture making that

Compositional study for the illustration in Jumanji *depicting a python coiled around a clock (see also pages 34 and 35).*

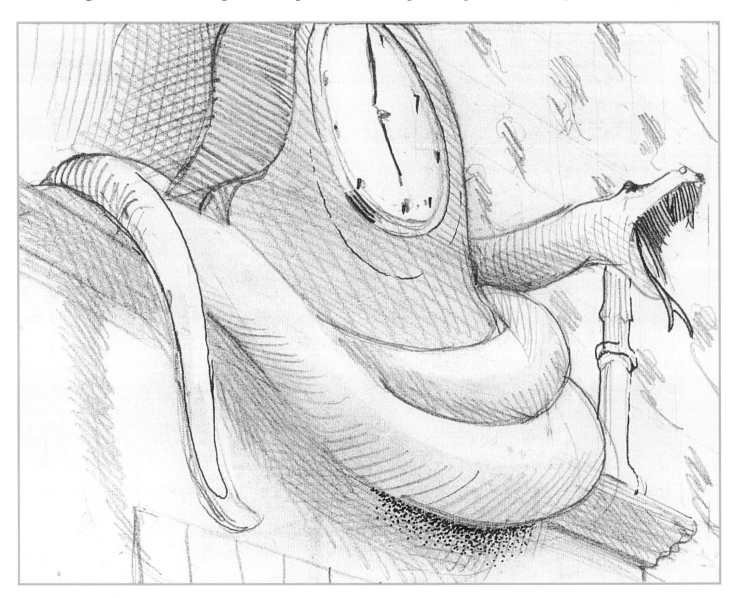

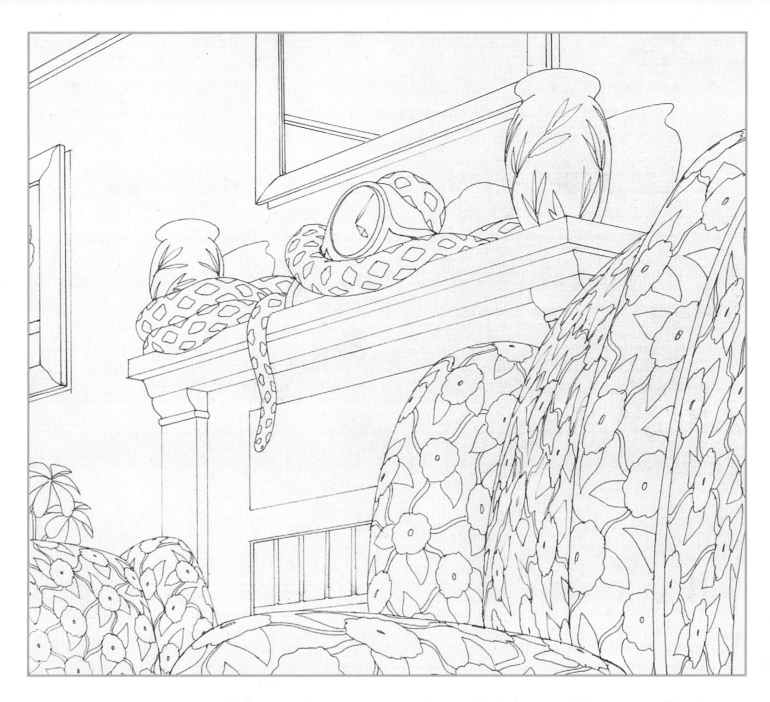

Detailed outline drawing (above) and final art (facing page) for the same scene.

gives me the most pleasure. I enjoy being able to move things around and to decide how big or small they should be.

"In the illustration on the jacket, for instance, I put the viewer in the room with the monkeys. But there are a thousand different vantage points from which to depict that scene. I could have drawn it looking over the girl's shoulder, showing what *she* saw through the open door. I drew the scene from close to floor level, looking up, which makes the monkeys look monumentally large. But I could also have drawn it from slightly higher up, looking across the monkeys' faces toward

the girl, and presented the scene from the monkeys' point of view." Van Allsburg showed his editor one or two of the first finished illustrations, then worked on his own until he'd finished.

"I like to draw from my imagination," Van Allsburg says. "The house depicted in *Jumanji* all came from my head." But in order to get lifelike drawings of animals and people, he sometimes also makes use of photographs or models. "Of course, I couldn't find pictures of monkeys in the exact poses I had chosen for my illustration. So I asked my wife to pose, and quickly drew her."

Drawing a believable image of the charging rhinos was especially tough, Van

Allsburg recalls, "because close-up photos of charging rhinos were nowhere to be found. That's when I started my collection of plastic animals."

Even when photos are available, however, Van Allsburg does not simply copy them. Instead, he says, "I have the photographs blown up fairly large and hang them up so far away in my studio that I can't see them very clearly. That way, as I draw from the photos, I also have to use my imagination."

Children of friends posed for Peter and Judy. "At the start of their adventures, Peter and Judy have to decide whether to rely on their parents or themselves. They choose themselves. So I picked as my models children with a serious, adult kind of look to them, children who looked as if they might make that choice."

Winning the Caldecott Medal, Van Allsburg says, "increased the size of my audience. I like knowing that a lot of people will see my work." The prize also helped change the way he viewed himself as an artist. "I was still making sculpture," he recalls, "and thought of myself as primarily a sculptor. But after having first received a Caldecott Honor for *The Garden of Abdul Gasazi* and then win-

Two preliminary drawings for the scene in which Judy and Peter are shown playing Jumanji. The outline drawing (facing page) is the closer of the two in composition to the finished illustration, which Van Allsburg drew as a mirror image of these studies.

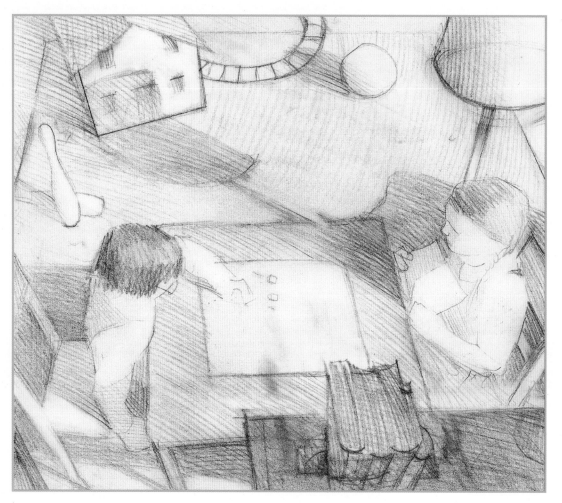

ning the medal back to back for *Jumanji*, I began to realize that maybe book illustration, not sculpture, was my true calling."

Van Allsburg has gone on to create many remarkable children's books and to teach illustration at the art school where he once studied, the Rhode Island School of Design (RISD—pronounced "RIZ-dee"—for short). In 1995 *Jumanji* also became a feature film, starring Robin Williams.

Van Allsburg receives many letters about his books. Readers of *Jumanji* most often want to know what happened to the Budwing boys, the children who get hold of the board game just as Peter and Judy's adventures come to an end. Other readers ask, as Van Allsburg recounts, "'why I illustrated the book in black and white.' Some children say they are amazed that the pictures *look* so much like color pictures, even though they're not. Others ask, 'Don't you have a box of crayons?' And some ask, 'Why would anyone do such a thing?'"

1980 *The Garden of Abdul Gasazi* (Houghton Mifflin), Caldecott Honor Book
1982 *Jumanji* (Houghton Mifflin), Caldecott Medal
1986 *The Polar Express* (Houghton Mifflin), Caldecott Medal

★ 1992 ★

Tuesday

BY

David Wiesner

(born February 5, 1956, Bridgewater, New Jersey)
Publisher: Clarion Books
Medium: watercolor

> A wordless book offers a different kind of experience. . . . Each viewer reads the book in his or her own way. . . . As a result, there are as many versions of what happened that Tuesday night as there are readers.
> — David Wiesner, Caldecott acceptance speech for *Tuesday*

*B*ecause my earlier books had been more serious, people didn't expect a book by me to be funny. So when I showed my dummy for *Tuesday* to my editor, Dorothy Briley, I didn't know how she would react. Dorothy took one look—and laughed! We sat around making pig and frog noises for a while. Then I went home and got right to work."

Early thumbnail sketch for the next-to-last illustration of Tuesday.

As a child growing up in suburban New Jersey, David Wiesner kept busy. He and his friends had "everything you could want—a brook, a cemetery, and a swamp" as backdrops for their outdoor adventures. They had walkie-talkies and knew a way of making "UFOs" that could actually be launched high into the air for mock invasions of Bridgewater.

At home, one of his favorite books contained drawings of dinosaurs rendered so realistically that for a time he believed them to be photographs. The class artist at school, he read—and copied pictures from—*Mad* magazine and action comics, including a series called *Nick Fury, Agent of SHIELD*, which featured wordless sequences of drawings. Wiesner found it fascinating to "read" pictures that told a story. In a high school film class he made silent movies. And as an undergraduate at the Rhode Island School of Design (RISD), he continued to find new ways of telling stories with pictures alone.

At RISD, Wiesner did not know at first what kind of art he wanted to do professionally. Because he enjoyed reading science fiction, he thought about illustrating the covers of sci-fi fantasies.

As it happened, two of Wiesner's favorite science fiction artists—Diane and Leo Dillon—also illustrated children's books, a field about which he knew very little. When a fellow student mentioned one day that the Dillons had just won their second Caldecott Medal (for *Ashanti to Zulu: African Traditions*, written by Margaret Musgrove, Dial, 1976), Wiesner first had to ask, "What is the Caldecott Medal?" Discovering that the Dillons illustrated children's books led Wiesner to wonder whether he might like to do so, too.

While at RISD, he met Trina Schart Hyman, an illustrator and the art director at *Cricket* magazine. (Hyman herself went on to win the 1985 Caldecott Medal for *Saint George and the Dragon*, retold by Margaret Hodges, published by Little, Brown, 1984). After seeing his artwork, she asked Wiesner to design a cover for *Cricket*. She also urged him to consider choosing children's book illustration as a career. With the help of Dilys Evans, another *Cricket* staff member who was just starting her own business as an artist's agent, Wiesner soon had more work as a children's book illustrator.

Over the next ten years Wiesner illustrated a variety of children's books, including the wordless *Free Fall* (1988) and *Hurricane* (1990). Both books received

Front and back cover illustration by Wiesner for the March 1989 issue of Cricket.

wide acclaim. Critics and fans praised his inventiveness and considerable skill as a painter. Wiesner hoped that another side of himself, his offbeat sense of humor, would one day also find its way into the art he made.

The idea for *Tuesday* grew out of Wiesner's second cover illustration for *Cricket*. The magazine asked him to choose between making a picture for Saint Patrick's Day and a picture about frogs. When he added a lily pad to one of his sketchbook drawings of frogs, something surprising—and magical—happened. Surrounded by white space, the lumpish creature looked to Wiesner as if it might be flying. A flying frog! A lily-pad magic carpet! He liked these ideas and knew when he turned in the *Cricket* cover that he was not finished with flying amphibians.

The next time he took out his sketchbook, the artist was himself airborne— bound for vacation aboard a commercial jetliner. "As I sat there and thought about the frogs," he recalls, "flashes of images came to me. I sketched rapidly: frogs rising out of the swamp, frogs flying through a clothesline, a man sitting at his kitchen table as frogs cruised past. In an hour it was all done. It was almost frightening how quickly it came to me!"

Page of the quick sketches Wiesner made, in midflight, when the idea for a book about flying frogs first occurred to him.

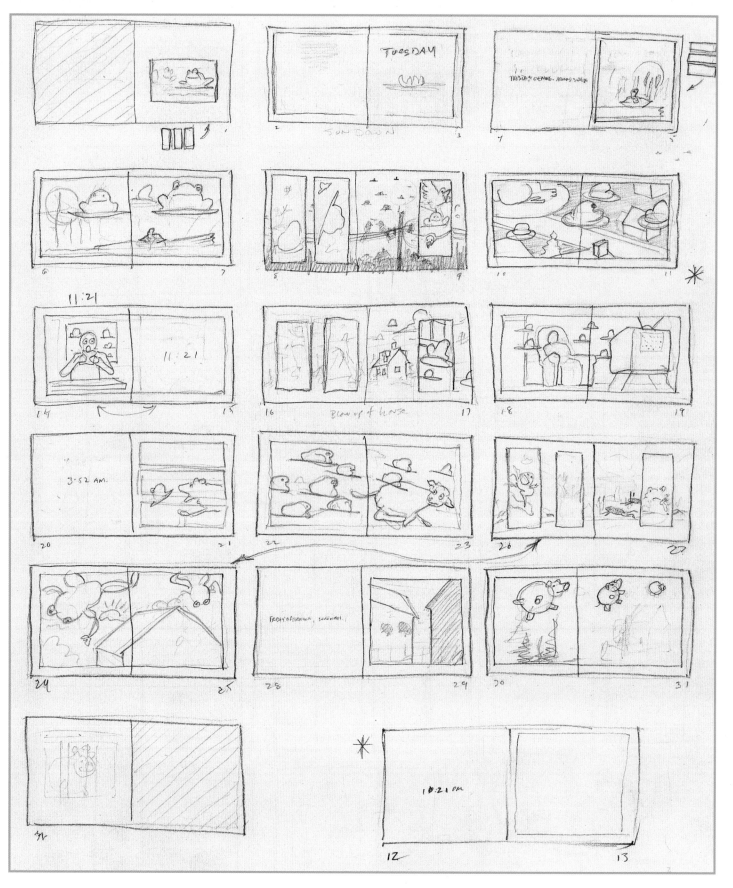

*This more detailed set of thumbnail drawings allowed Wiesner to see the
entire book at a glance and to rethink the sequencing of the illustrations.*

Based on these sketches, he prepared the dummy that made his editor laugh. Dorothy Briley had a few suggestions for making the book even funnier. It was her idea, for instance, to devote a big double-page illustration to the tongue-in-cheek scene near the end in which the police and a TV crew try in vain to figure out what mysterious doings have occurred overnight in their peaceful town.

Using the dummy as his guide, he made detailed drawings of each scene, then traced the drawings onto watercolor paper and painted the finished illustrations.

Double-page spread from the dummy Wiesner prepared to show Dorothy Briley (top). Wiesner used the more detailed drawing of the same scene (bottom) for tracing onto watercolor paper.

During the course of his work, Wiesner studied nature photos from *National Geographic* and sculpted a frog model in clay. He knew that the more realistic he made his paintings, the stranger and funnier his frog invasion would seem. He chose himself as the model for the young man enjoying a late-night snack because, he recalls, "I just felt that I *had* to be in the middle of this story."

Wiesner wanted a title that highlighted the story's time element. He chose *Tuesday* in part because it sounded like "Ooze Day," which seemed right for a book about frogs.

Tuesday proved to be a success with the critics. Teachers liked it too, and began asking their grade school students to write and draw their own stories based on Wiesner's wordless original. "I received hundreds of *Next Tuesday*s—the children's sequels to my book. They're very funny."

Wiesner, who lived in Brooklyn, New York, at the time, was at home just starting his work day one January morning when the chairperson of the Caldecott Committee telephoned to say he had won the medal. At first the soft-spoken artist didn't know what to say in response. Then he became unusually chatty. He thanked the librarian, phoned his wife and editor, and accepted an invitation to

Clay model made by the artist.

Final watercolor art.

appear on the *Today* show the following morning. When things calmed down a bit, Wiesner, still alone in his studio, sat back and listened to a tape of a favorite rock and roll group, the Ramones, turned up full blast. For all the day's excitement, he even managed to do some work. Wiesner later thought how lucky he was to have been halfway through his next book, *June 29, 1999* (1992), when news came of the Caldecott Medal for *Tuesday*. People who have won a prize sometimes worry about having to top themselves—"What's Mr. Caldecott Medal going to do next?" as Wiesner says with a laugh. Having a new book on its way freed him from much of the worry.

He felt especially proud to have received the prize the year after one of his favorite RISD teachers, David Macaulay, won the medal for *Black and White* (Houghton Mifflin, 1990). "I *really* knew what winning the Caldecott meant to me when I saw the American Library Association's large poster showing the jackets of every book that has received the medal since 1938. When I saw my book and name at the end of the list, I thought, 'Wow!'—and realized that from now on I would always be a part of that tradition."

1989 *Free Fall* (Lothrop, Lee and Shepard), Caldecott Honor Book
1992 *Tuesday* (Clarion Books), Caldecott Medal

1938 *Animals of the Bible, a Picture Book*. Text selected by Helen Dean Fish. Illustrated by Dorothy P. Lathrop. Lippincott.

1939 *Mei Li*. Written and Illustrated by Thomas Handforth. Doubleday.

1940 *Abraham Lincoln*. Written and Illustrated by Ingri and Edgar Parin d'Aulaire. Doubleday.

1941 *They Were Strong and Good*. Written and Illustrated by Robert Lawson. Viking.

1942 *Make Way for Ducklings*. Written and Illustrated by Robert McCloskey. Viking.

1943 *The Little House*. Written and Illustrated by Virginia Lee Burton. Houghton.

1944 *Many Moons*. Written by James Thurber. Illustrated by Louis Slobodkin. Harcourt.

1945 *Prayer for a Child*. Written by Rachel Field. Illustrated by Elizabeth Orton Jones. Macmillan.

1946 *The Rooster Crows*: *A Book of American Rhymes and Jingles*. Compiled and Illustrated by Maud and Miska Petersham. Macmillan.

1947 *The Little Island*. Written by Golden MacDonald, pseud. (Margaret Wise Brown). Illustrated by Leonard Weisgard. Doubleday.

1948 *White Snow, Bright Snow*. Written by Alvin Tresselt. Illustrated by Roger Duvoisin. Lothrop.

1949 *The Big Snow*. Written and Illustrated by Berta and Elmer Hader. Macmillan.

1950 *Song of the Swallows*. Written and Illustrated by Leo Politi. Scribner.

1951 *The Egg Tree*. Written and Illustrated by Katherine Milhous. Scribner.

1952 *Finders Keepers*. Written by Will, pseud. (William Lipkind). Illustrated by Nicolas, pseud. (Nicolas Mordvinoff). Harcourt.

1953 *The Biggest Bear*. Written and Illustrated by Lynd Ward. Houghton.

1954 *Madeline's Rescue*. Written and Illustrated by Ludwig Bemelmans. Viking.

1955 *Cinderella; or, The Little Glass Slipper*. Illustrated and translated from Charles Perrault's French text by Marcia Brown. Scribner.

1956 *Frog Went A-Courtin'*. Retold by John Langstaff. Illustrated by Feodor Rojankovsky. Harcourt.

1957 *A Tree Is Nice*. Written by Janice May Udry. Illustrated by Marc Simont. Harper.

1958 *Time of Wonder*. Written and Illustrated by Robert McCloskey. Viking.

1959 *Chanticleer and the Fox*. Adapted from Chaucer's *Canterbury Tales* and Illustrated by Barbara Cooney. Crowell.

1960 *Nine Days to Christmas*. Written by Marie Hall Ets and Aurora Labastida. Illustrated by Marie Hall Ets. Viking.

1961 *Baboushka and the Three Kings*. Written by Ruth Robbins. Illustrated by Nicolas Sidjakov. Parnassus.

1962 *Once a Mouse*. Retold and Illustrated by Marcia Brown. Scribner.

1963 *The Snowy Day*. Written and Illustrated by Ezra Jack Keats. Viking.

1964 *Where the Wild Things Are*. Written and Illustrated by Maurice Sendak. Harper.

1965 *May I Bring a Friend?* Written by Beatrice Schenk de Regniers. Illustrated by Beni Montresor. Atheneum.

1966 *Always Room for One More*. Written by Sorche Nic Leodhas, pseud. (Leclaire Alger). Illustrated by Nonny Hogrogian. Holt.

1967 *Sam, Bangs & Moonshine*. Written and Illustrated by Evaline Ness. Holt.

1968 *Drummer Hoff*. Written by Barbara Emberley. Illustrated by Ed Emberley. Prentice-Hall.

1969 *The Fool of the World and the Flying Ship*. Retold by Arthur Ransome. Illustrated by Uri Shulevitz. Farrar.

1970 *Sylvester and the Magic Pebble*. Written and Illustrated by William Steig. Windmill.

1971 *A Story A Story*. Retold and illustrated by Gail E. Haley. Atheneum.

1972 *One Fine Day*. Retold and Illustrated by Nonny Hogrogian. Macmillan.

1973 *The Funny Little Woman*. Retold by Arlene Mosel. Illustrated by Blair Lent. Dutton.

1974 *Duffy and the Devil*. Retold by Harve Zemach. Illustrated by Margot Zemach. Farrar.

1975 *Arrow to the Sun*. Adapted and Illustrated by Gerald McDermott. Viking.

1976 *Why Mosquitoes Buzz in People's Ears*. Retold by Verna Aardema. Illustrated by Leo and Diane Dillon. Dial.

1977 *Ashanti to Zulu: African Traditions*. Written by Margaret Musgrove. Illustrated by Leo and Diane Dillon. Dial.

1978 *Noah's Ark*. Illustrated by Peter Spier. Doubleday.

1979 *The Girl Who Loved Wild Horses*. Written and Illustrated by Paul Goble. Bradbury.

1980 *Ox-Cart Man*. Written by Donald Hall. Illustrated by Barbara Cooney. Viking.

1981 *Fables*. Written and Illustrated by Arnold Lobel. Harper.

1982 *Jumanji*. Written and Illustrated by Chris Van Allsburg. Houghton.

1983 *Shadow*. Written by Blaise Cendrars. Translated and Illustrated by Marcia Brown. Scribner.

1984 *The Glorious Flight: Across the Channel with Louis Blériot*. Written and Illustrated by Alice and Martin Provensen. Viking.

1985 *Saint George and the Dragon*. Retold by Margaret Hodges. Illustrated by Trina Schart Hyman. Little, Brown.

1986 *The Polar Express*. Written and Illustrated by Chris Van Allsburg. Houghton.

1987 *Hey, Al*. Written by Arthur Yorinks. Illustrated by Richard Egielski. Farrar.

1988 *Owl Moon*. Written by Jane Yolen. Illustrated by John Schoenherr. Philomel.

1989 *Song and Dance Man*. Written by Karen Ackerman. Illustrated by Stephen Gammell. Knopf.

1990 *Lon Po Po: A Red-Riding Hood Story from China*. Written and Illustrated by Ed Young. Philomel.

1991 *Black and White*. Written and Illustrated by David Macaulay. Houghton.

1992 *Tuesday*. Written and Illustrated by David Wiesner. Clarion.

1993 *Mirette on the High Wire*. Written and Illustrated by Emily Arnold McCully. Putnam.

1994 *Grandfather's Journey*. Written and Illustrated by Allen Say. Houghton.

1995 *Smoky Night*. Written by Eve Bunting. Illustrated by David Diaz. Harcourt.

1996 *Officer Buckle and Gloria*. Written and Illustrated by Peggy Rathmann. Putnam.

1997 *Golem*. Written and Illustrated by David Wisniewski. Clarion.

1998 *Rapunzel*. Retold and Illustrated by Paul O. Zelinsky. Dutton.